This is for Liani Spriggs, who gave me motivation when I wanted to give up.

This is for Gwendolyn Swinton (R.I.P.), my Mama. I just want to make you proud.

This is for my therapist Dr. Cymer, who taught me not to be so hard on myself and appreciate the small things.

This is for Jaquci and Andrew Cowles for giving me the opportunity at your greenhouse.

This is for Tammy Road and Judy Gillan, for believing that this city girl from the projects could work on my own farm.

This is for my middle school teacher Mr. Brent Northup for being the first to read and edit my book. What an honor.

This is for my secret gardens all over the world.

This is for all my customers I met along the way at farmers markets.

Thank you all.

Table of Contents

Sunrise

Tofu Scramble..........27
Pancake Skewer..........27
Breakfast Potato..........30
Avocado Toast..........30
Fruit Bowl..........31
French Toast........31
Cheese Grits with Sauteed Vegetables..........32
PBC (peanut butter, bananas and chocolate)..........32
Stuffed Apples..........33
Sweet Potato Pancake..............33
No Bake Peanut Butter Oatmeal Ball..........35
Overnight Oats..........35

Chip n Dip

Black Bean Salsa..........37
Hummus..........37
Mango Salsa..........39
Simple Guacamole..........39
Spinach & Artichoke..........39

Grass Fed

Avocado Salad..........41
Cranberry Apple Salad..........41
Swiss Chard Boat Salad..........42
Chick 'n' less Salad w/ Raspberry Vinaigrette Dressing..........42
Cucumber Salad..........43
Eggless Potato Salad..........43
Fancy Salad..........44
Strawberry Kiwi Salad w/ Strawberry Vinaigrette Dressing..........44
Taco Salad..........46
Veggie Pasta Salad..........46

Wrap It Up

Sundown

Sweet Tooth

About Us, Our Vegan Journey

Growing up I always had a thing for cooking, especially growing up in the same house with a mother and a southern grandma who were great cooks. Every day after school dinner was ready. Sundays we had a big dinner together, sometimes with guests. Years later, after my grandmother and my mother had passed, I followed in their footsteps, cooking for my siblings and my daughter. In 2015 I was faced with some tough financial and health issues that would change my life. My health affected my job, and after 3 years they were ready to let me go. I had given the company time on holidays, including Christmas, and I had given up many family events for work. It was time to reevaluate my future and do some soul searching.

Meanwhile my daughter Liani was suffering with acid reflux. At only 14 years old she was afraid of taking medication for the rest of her life. Little did I know she had researched natural remedies and she decided to become vegan. She discovered that veganism dates back to 1944, when Donald Watson first coined the term"vegan" to describe the doctrine that man should live without exploiting animals. When I asked how I could support her lifestyle change, she replied "I need to go to Whole Foods." Her first grocery store trip as vegan inspired me to do "Meatless Monday" each week, to show her I was open to her change and I was willing to give up meat one day a week.

Later that year she began to lose interest in school and in socializing due to her lifestyle change. School offered no vegan options at lunch, frustrating a high school student that wanted to be healthy. I tried to do everything in my power to change school lunches, which were full of processed foods and sugar junk. I contacted the food service company, which gave me the run-around. They told me they had to have a source of protein on a salad, like ham or turkey. They used the food pyramid to justify why my daughter couldn't get a plain salad! To the school, I suggested we start a small garden to provide fresh produce, for not only the kids that were vegan, but the families who might have run into hard times and needed some assistance.

There was city funding in the budget to start gardens in public schools, but my child's school didn't qualify for it because it's a charter school. I offered my time and resources to help create a school garden. The idea was to start in grades k-5, saving milk containers and cartons to start seeds in. I remembered when I was small in school we planted seeds that way for Mother's Day gifts.

After what I thought was a successful first meeting at the school, I got no response. Liani began to hate school more. Mothers do everything we can to help and protect our children, so again I met with school officials to address my concerns. At that meeting I was told to have her bring her own lunch because of school policies.

Another issue was contributing to my daughter's increasing alienation from her school. She was being told that the only way she would be successful was by attending college, that she needed more years of what she was coming to hate. Liani and I had a long heart-to-heart conversation about her future and how we could deal with these challenges. She had done research on homeschooling, and after I did mine we agreed she would exit public school. She started high school online.

As we began that study, part of her homework was to watch documentaries, and I recommend them to you (you can find these on Netflix):

"What the Health"
"Forks over Knives"
"Vegucated"
"Cows-piracy"
"Rotten"

In September that year, a sandwich shop in Brooklyn, New York got me thinking seriously about growing my own produce. On a visit to my Brooklyn aunt, she took us to that very nice shop, which had fresh local food, juices and a variety of baked goods. At that time I was having some health issues of my own, so the idea to grow my food was growing on me.

To support Liani, we celebrated our first vegan Thanksgiving. Though we were used to the traditional foods for the holiday, this time it would be different. Thanksgiving dinner normally took all day to cook. Our vegan dinner took 2 hours, and I can say our first Thanksgiving was successful!

Happy New Year! And it was, but my health was a continuing problem. After many trips to doctors, the dermatologist, pulmonologist, neurologist, a polysomnogram study and ear nose and throat tests, I finally found the problem. I had allergies and respiratory issues that were out of control. I underwent respiratory surgery.

I also noticed that changing my diet by eliminating dairy helped with my allergies and overall health. That and the fact that I often felt sick after eating meat led me to think a lot about becoming vegan. It was a difficult decision because it was a lifestyle change away from everything I knew, but I was ready.

I saw a nutritionist, Rebecca, to check all my nutrition levels before transitioning. I discovered I had a vitamin D deficiency. Rebecca and I worked to eliminate high fructose syrup, artificial colors and flavors, and gluten. I set a timer to snack every three hours, I didn't eat after 7:00 pm and I remembered to drink plenty of water, "must do" instructions from the nutritionist.

I started to gain a different perspective on what I had been eating. Grocery shopping that used to take 30 minutes took three hours, because I was required to read labels. I learned to shop for fresh produce, fruit, and natural organic foods. Upon returning to the nutritionist with my homework completed, I weighed in and found out I had dropped 10 pounds without trying. I would continue to see Rebecca for the next few months.

2016 was a big year. We started shopping from an online store, Thrive Market, which offered vegan items that were not available nearby. In April we attended an event that offered many vegan options, and we attended every workshop we could. I read a book called "Unleash the Inner Healing Power of Foods," by Frank K. Wood, which led me to start food shopping in more local businesses and eating more fresh foods. I began purchasing from local farms, Asian markets and family owned stores, instead of big corporations.

In May of that year Liani and I started our vegan business. We called it "2 Cents Homegrown." The nickname "2 Cents" had been given to my late mother by her brother because he said she had outgrown her original name, Penny. We began to grow our own produce in our very own backyard. Friends and family joined me on August 12, 2016 to launch our business and sample baked goods and homemade dips.

We attended our first two farmers markets as vendors. I received my allergen certification after attending an annual client networking event. I taught myself how to make soap. I even tried to host workshops in my community, in what was known as the "Maker's Space," but people just didn't seem interested in healthy eating, at least not in my city. It was a good lesson, teaching us to keep our heads up and keep going forward.

Then in September I took a long overdue trip to California to surprise my dad for his 50th birthday, and I made time to see the wonderful farmers markets there. There I was even more convinced that this was our calling, mother and daughter, to promote veganism. One of the California farmers markets had a cool yogurt bar that had vegan options, and I knew I could get used to this lifestyle. I returned home with some pecan brittle, bath bombs and soaps. Now back home with a new outlook on veganism from the west coast, I was inspired to get in the kitchen.

There were limited vegan restaurant options where we lived. For us to go out to eat required at least a 30 minute drive. That meant more cooking at home, and eating out would be considered a treat.

Soon after I began to prepare my body to permanently become vegan. I took an aerial yoga class, and all the foods I had grown to love, like chicken and cheese, had to exit my system; I was leaving them behind.

Happy New Vegan! 2017 started rough with my body detoxing. I experienced fatigue, cold sweats and weakness. I made sure to drink plenty of fluids and to snack every three hours. I also began to realize how much it would change my social life, my relationships and even my family interactions. I had never looked at how many events, such as birthday parties, weddings and holidays, revolve around food. This meant more planning when I was invited out, because there were very few people I knew that ate healthy, let alone vegan. My daughter and I now had to either eat before we left home or be sure to travel with snacks. Now of course we would get the 21 questions, like "What do you eat?" and "Where do you get your protein?" This change in my life changed my social circles completely. I understood better what Liani had experienced when she became vegan. I stayed home more than I went out, and I was ok with that. We decided to join more vegan social groups and we continued our research to create more delicious meals with our homegrown produce.

In March of that year I decided to get rid of all my animal products, such as leather boots, purses and beauty care products. Hungry to learn more, I started looking for jobs in agriculture to get more hands-on training, and I got accepted into a farming school. This vegan life was beginning to open new doors, including a job at a greenhouse farm. I got the opportunity to take a tour of a CDC (Center for Disease Control) kitchen. I was thinking about more production and more locations, to network and get our business out there. My first event was in March, selling our vegan cookies, soaps and scrubs. This was great exposure for us and we sold out! Earth Day was approaching and there were many events to choose from. We planned to do the Earth Day Extravaganza in Enfield, Connecticut in April, which put our company in the Hartford Courant newspaper.

We traveled to New York City in June to the Vegan Street Fair, to reward ourselves for our hard work. It was a hot day, my tolerance of the humidity helped me realize I was in good shape! I saw there was a need for vegan foods and people will travel to get it. We set out to find more events for vegans, which brought us to the Compassionfest in late July. There we networked with other vegans and got a great response to our small business. In late September we started participating at a farmers market located at Springfield Technical Community College. There I built relationships with several good vendors. We celebrated our second vegan Thanksgiving and we sold dry cookie dough mixes for the holiday season.

Happy 2nd Veganversary to me! My first few years taught me a lot. I got accepted into a small farm dream course for which I had been on a waiting list. We got more creative by offering a juice program. Things were starting to fall into place. I lectured a class at Elms College, and a city health clinic had me host a workshop. I took a PSA (Produce Safety Alliance) grower training course and I was approved to take a WIC (Women In Child) supplemental nutrition program for women and their children. WIC is a federal food and nutrition service of the US Department of Agriculture for the health of new mothers who are breastfeeding, low-income pregnant women and children under five. SNAP (Supplemental Nutrition Assistance Program) provides assistance for low-income to no-income people living in the US to purchase food. After taking those classes, I can accept these forms of payment at our farmers market table. I am happy to promote programs like these, which encourage low-income mothers to eat and feed their children in more healthy ways.

Balancing school, work, home and single parenting sure wasn't easy but I loved every part of it. I continued to take any course, any class that would advance my skills and knowledge. I joined NESFI (New England Small Farm Institute) a non-profit organization with a mission to promote small start-up farms in the beginning and transitioning stages, by training and providing informational sessions. I sub-leased ⅓ acre of farming land, and I taught myself how to make skin care products in addition to soap, like facial scrubs, bath bombs and lip balm. I grow flowers and incorporate them into everything I sell.

I keep busy paying the bills and increasing profits. I found the perfect position for myself at the Big E, the New England states fair, and one of the biggest fairs in the nation, as a manager of the Wine and Cheese Barn. In that position I am able to network, have fun and get paid while doing it. During the fair I created a detox drink that is a great liver cleanse. When the fair was over, it was time to prepare for the holiday season, and what better way than with an infused sweet potato pie, a holiday vegan gift basket or a bottle of coquito? Oh, and don't forget your moisturizing soaps for the winter!

Happy three-year veganversary! I applaud myself because, as you might find, it has been quite an experience, a journey that has required a lot of discipline. Veganism has changed my social life, my relationships, my mindset and the way I see the world I had come to question. I love the person I'm becoming, and I'm excited, choosing events to attend and making plans to grow my business.

I went to Atlanta on book business, and I noticed how far behind the times my hometown is in healthy eating and veganism. There were abundant vegan options in restaurants and grocery stores there, and I felt like I was where I needed to be, a place where I could write and experiment in the kitchen.

I wondered why there isn't more written about the mental, emotional and social challenges that come with becoming vegan, and I decided to make that a part of this book, to help people through it. My time in Atlanta ended when I returned home for a family funeral.

Book plans would be delayed and extended again. I continued my education with a cooking class, and I returned to my farming "roots." By June I once again prepared the land and planted my crops of vegetables. Before the Big E opened I took the time to reconnect with one of my old English teachers, who helped me edit my first book draft. By that time, I realized that I hadn't been seeing the same friends I did before, and I was going to fewer family functions, but it was ok. I felt in my heart I was in the right place.

My first event that year was in July, and doubt began to creep into my head, something that happens often in transitioning to healthy eating, and more often in people who start a business from scratch and attempt to write a book. I overcame doubt and I managed to gain access to a commercial space, a step forward to do more business.

Like all farmers, I am dependent on weather conditions, and that summer a hailstorm cut my growing season short. I saved everything I could, sold what I could and preserved what I could in sauces, pickles and dried herbs for seasoning or tea. I composted what was left. It was time to think about indoor farming, a hoop house or greenhouse to have a longer growing season.

If you ever write a book or start a business, you will probably experience setting it aside for a while, to regroup, rethink and reflect. That was my time heading into the winter that year. It helped me in my determination to keep going, to refuse to fail, to share with the world the story of a flower child who spent years searching, and finally found herself.

Do you know what USRDA stands for?

USRDA: United States Recommended Daily Allowance, the daily amount of protein, vitamins and minerals that the FDA has established is sufficient to maintain the nutritional health of persons in age groups and categories. These recommendations are developed by the Food and Nutrition Board of the National Academy of Sciences and are used in the nutritional labelings of foods. Information that must be on food labels includes company name, address, phone, serving size, calories, and nutrients information. Foods such as crabmeat have to be labeled as an imitation/substitute food because they are often not the real thing. Enriched food means there are nutrients that are lost during processing and have been added back. Almost every food process lessens the amount of nutrients that are in food because of exposure to high levels of heat, oxygen and light.

Basic Food "Pyramid" and Recommended Daily Quantities

There are 6 food groups: Grains 6-11 servings
                         Vegetable 3-5 servings
                         Fruit 2-4 servings
                         Milk and Cheese 2-3 servings
                         Meat/ Beans 2-3 servings
Oils are not a food but can be used sparingly and they are featured because they contribute vitamin E and fatty acids - 4 teaspoons (according to the 1992 food guide pyramid).

Grains such as whole wheat flour, oatmeal, brown rice and whole cornmeal contribute niacin, riboflavin, thiamin, iron, magnesium, and potassium fiber. Vegetables such as lettuce, spinach, corn, potato and carrot contribute folate, potassium, fiber, vitamins A, C, K, E and magnesium. Fruits such as apples, bananas, grapefruit, grapes, mangoes, oranges, peaches and plums contribute folate, potassium, fiber and vitamins A and C. Ice cream and soy milk contribute protein, riboflavin, calcium and vitamins A and C. Monounsaturated fats, such as peanut oil, are oils from vegetable products that are liquid at room temperature.

With a proper diet we can reduce the rates of many health problems, such as low infant birth weight and preterm births, iron deficiency, adult osteoporosis and new cases of diabetes. Cariogenic foods like cakes, doughnuts, and pastries are consumed in great quantities by Americans, and the damage they do is often not realized until it's too late. Non-cariogenic foods include whole grain muffins, popcorn and baked light chips. Refined sugars are a part of Americans' unhealthy average daily intake of 125 grams of sucrose and 50 grams of corn syrup. Fiber plays a very important part of our digestive system and helps lower cholesterol. Zinc is necessary for a biochemical reaction that helps the immune system function properly. Iron is used to carry oxygen in the blood. Fresh ingredients lower sodium, and oils provide essential nutrients.

Improve Your Health With a Healthy Diet

One way to improve your overall health is by getting the proper vitamins. Vitamins are organic compounds that are vital to life and indispensable to body functions.

Vitamin A - vision, maintenance of the inner and outer skin, immune defenses, growth of bones and body, and normal development of cells. Animal food sources include liver and fish oil. To a vegan, good sources of vitamin A are carrots, sweet potatoes, kale and broccoli. A deficiency of vitamin A can lead to night blindness and loss of appetite.

Vitamin B1 - helps the body metabolize carbohydrates, lipids and amino acids, helps with the breakdown of fat and proteins, and keeps mucus membranes healthy. Deficiency can cause lack of energy and irritability.

Vitamin B6 - aids in the conversion of the amino acid tryptophan to niacin (vitamin B3), has a role in immune function and steroid hormone activity, assists in releasing stored glucose from glycogen, and contributes to regulate blood glucose. Deficiency symptoms are weakness, psychological depression, confusion, irritability and insomnia. Good food sources of vitamin B6 are leafy greens, vegetables and fruits.

Vitamin B12 - helps maintain the sheaths that surround and protect nerve fibers. Deficiency symptoms are anemia, smooth tongue, tingling numbness and fatigue. It has been proven that changing to a plant-based lifestyle can reverse that deficiency.

Vitamin C - works on forming and maintaining connective tissues, and as a powerful antioxidant. Food sources include fresh fruits, raw and cooked vegetables. Deficiency symptoms are loss of appetite, bleeding gums, loss of teeth, swollen ankles and wrists.

Vitamin D - plays a major role in preserving phosphorus levels in the blood and is extremely important in maintaining healthy bones. Lack of vitamin D can cause our kidneys to overwork.

Vitamin E- An antioxidant, acts as a bodyguard and protects eyesight

Vitamin K - to activate proteins that help clot the blood. Good food sources are dark greens, leafy vegetables, lettuces, broccoli, brussel sprouts and cabbage.

Credit of this information was learned in health class in college

Cleaning the Body

I recommend doing a detox before any diet or life change related to food. People who are vegan find it useful to detox the body occasionally, for maintenance of good health. It's a great way to remove toxins, reboot and recharge your body. Detoxification is a normal body process to eliminate toxins in the colon and liver.

There are three good opportunities to detox: 1) When transitioning to a healthier lifestyle; 2) It's great in the spring when the body is coming out of the "hibernation" of winter; and 3) After taking medication that has caused your energy levels to shift. Do a seven day or a 14 day detox to get you back on track. You should drink a glass of water every two hours, totaling about a gallon, so you will feel less hungry. You might notice as the body gets lighter and lighter, you become more aware of your body. It's getting rid of toxins that have accumulated over time.

With a juicing detox, the body has no carbohydrates to burn for energy, so it burns stored fats wherever they are available. Detoxing the body has some side effects you might expect. People have felt weak, and light headed, and some reported a smell from the bad toxins seeping from the skin. The pounds lost with juicing can be put back on quickly if we're not careful, because most of it is water weight.

The three ingredients I use in my detox drink are:
1. Turmeric – digest fats, reduce bloating
2. Lemon - cleanse liver and reduce muscle pain
3. Ginger - weight loss and digestion

Mix 1 tablespoon turmeric, 1 tablespoon fresh ginger, 2 squeezed lemons and 1 gallon water Drink one every morning for seven days, refilling the glass 6-8 times a day. Results can vary, depending on what you're still putting in your body. For example, someone who eats beef will have different results than someone who eats just fish, because beef takes about a week to digest.

Mucoid Plaque Cleanse

This cleanse will help get rid of mucus, which is an unpleasant waste, often eliminated through colon irrigation (enemas to clean the lower intestines). There is also good mucus that helps protect and defend our airways.

The cleanse is a mixture of a common laxative psyllium husk, bentonite clay, which acts as a detoxifier, and cascara sagrada, another laxative. Mix the clay and husk together in apple cider or distilled water and drink 2x to 3x a day, an hour before eating, and take the cascara sagrada at night (only taken the first seven days of cleanse). This cleanse is recommended for 14 days and 4 times a year, once each season.

Prior to starting this detox I recommend giving up red meat, pork, take out food and all processed foods (if you are not vegan already). There are simple ways that will help gear toward a diet of raw fruits and vegetables, which will help reduce mucus in the body. Try to avoid "mucus foods" which include corn, dairy, red meat, eggs, bread, soy, caffeine, wine, wheat and sunflower. Foods that reduce mucus are pumpkins, grapefruit, watercress, pickles, onions, broth, chamomile, cayenne pepper, agar, garlic and olive oil.

The Benefits of Water

Warm Water
> Helps flush kidney and improve bowel movements
> Can help with hangover
> Allows better hydration

Cold Water
> Cools your body after workout
> 2 glasses of water upon waking up helps activate organs
> 1 glass before eating helps digestion
> 1 glass before a shower helps lower blood pressure
> 1 16 oz glass of water and 1 key lime will help with acid reflux and prevent constipation and other stomach issues. It also helps remove mucus
> One negative effect - cold water solidifies fats from food, making it harder for the body to digest

Drink a gallon a day, and here are a few ways to make it fun!

Infused water is fruit, vegetables, herbs or combinations of all soaked for 24-48 hours, adding natural flavors to water without any sugar. Use seltzer if you like fizz. You can also freeze some in your ice tray. Here are some great infusion ideas:

> cucumber, lemon, strawberry and apple cider vinegar
> blueberries and cucumber
> lemon, lime, strawberry and mint
> lemon balm, strawberry and mint
> lemon, raspberry, rosemary
> spearmint and cucumber
> kiwi and raspberry
> grapefruit slices
> fresh ginger, turmeric, apple cider vinegar and cayenne pepper

Helpful food facts for skin, hair and overall health

- Catnip tea, which is commonly used to treat anxiety, nervousness and other symptoms such as cramping, insomnia and indigestion.
- Eating three dates everyday will improve digestion, help relieve allergies, increase iron levels and boost energy.
- Elderberrys help break up mucus in the body.
- Ginger root helps with nausea, migraines and cramping.
- Almond oil and honey (agave) can help prevent dark circles and eye bags. Dark circles under eyes are related to iron deficiency, not getting enough in your diet to make the right amount of red blood cells that the body needs.
- Sliced potatoes, place on facial dark spots and leave on face for 5mins. Then wash in lukewarm water, pat dry and apply hydrating cream.
- Mix pineapple juice and turmeric together to make a paste. Apply to eyes for 20 minutes every day for 2 weeks.
- Burdock root helps treat eczema and other skin conditions.
- Jamaican black castor oil can help increase hair growth.
- Pepper gender is determined by flipping it over. If it has 4 bumps it's a female which will be full of seeds and is better for eating raw. The male will have three bumps and is less sweet, making it better for cooking.
- Rose water helps hydrate, lighten and tighten the skin.
- Used tea bags can be put in the freezer for 20 mins and placed under eyes to help puffiness.
- 2 teaspoons of chia seeds is 32% of your daily magnesium and five times more calcium than milk.

Know where your food comes from

Try going to local farmers markets and farms in season for the best quality produce. You will be able to question the farmers on their growing techniques, such as chemical use and spraying. The produce there is not the same as in grocery stores, which store their produce in refrigerated trucks for days before they reach the shelves. Off season it's ok to buy frozen produce and fruit, or even cans which you can purchase from your local dollar store. Believe it or not, both canned and frozen carry the same nutrients, because all produce loses some value once picked from the plant, whether they're housed in plastic or metal cans. I learned to preserve my vegetables by canning them so I can enjoy them over the winter months. Save some money by shopping weekly to catch savings because it's very unlikely for vegan and natural foods to be on sale. This also keeps food fresh and is less wasteful. Discount and family owned stores are great places to shop; it lets the money go back to the community instead of the corporations. You may want to see what wholesalers have in bulk when it comes to pasta, dry and canned goods, and invest in it if you eat a lot of it.

Sweet Self Reliance

You can become more self-sufficient by growing your own foods and making your own beauty products. After a focus on what you put into your body, perhaps it's time to look at what you put on your body. After researching and watching countless hours of videos I started making my own soap, exfoliating scrubs, lip balm, bath salts and bath bombs. I found how simple they were to make with everyday ingredients I was already familiar with, and were in my own kitchen. Most of your daily beauty products contain chemicals that are very harmful. Try picking up your favorite body spray or lotion and google every ingredient. And how about your child's fruit snack? Pretty disturbing! Once you know about harmful ingredients, it's hard to act like you don't.

Try to buy food and beauty products with at least seven natural ingredients that you can read. Many health issues are caused by the foods and chemicals we are putting in and on our bodies.

Healthy Vegan Substitutes

For Egg - banana, chia seeds, tofu, applesauce when baking
Meat - tofu, lentils, walnuts
Milk - cashews, almonds, soy, coconut, rice, oatmeal
Cheese - cashew, almond, nutritional yeast, carrot, potato, onion
Rice - cauliflower
Bread - chard, lettuce, cauliflower
Bacon - eggplant, tempeh
Pasta - squash, zucchini
Tuna - garbanzo bean, tofu
Beef - beans, kale,

Keep Your Foods Fresh!

Foods That Don't Require Refrigeration:

apple, avocado, banana, kiwi, lemons, oranges, peaches and papayas;
cucumbers, eggplant, garlic, ginger, peppers, potatoes, tomatoes, pumpkins

Require Refrigeration:

blackberries, strawberries, blueberries, raspberries, cherries, grapes and figs;
carrots, celery, broccoli, radish, spinach, cabbage;
fruit and vegetables once cut should be refrigerated

Kitchen Must-Haves

Spices
Black pepper
Red pepper flakes
Onion powder
Basil
Nutritional yeast
Mint
Old bay
Pink himalaya sea salt
Imitation bacon bits

Kitchen tools
Slate cutting board
Can opener
Food processor
Blender
Cooling rack
Wooden spoon
Cutting knife
Mixing bowl
Spice rack
Baking pan
Dehydrator
Serving tray
Whisk
Flour sifter

Baking
Apple sauce
Brown sugar
Baking soda and powder
Cinnamon
Cocoa powder
Coconut oil
Chocolate chips
Flax seeds
Flax flour

Flour (oat, almond, pastry)

Foods
Avocado
Banana
Beans
Black rice
Cereal
Corn
Garlic
Grain bread
Grape oil
Lettuce
Onion
Pasta
Potatoes
Noodles
Fruit - in season or frozen

Refrigerated
Seitan (wheat gluten, a good meat substitute)
Vegan butter
Tofu
Plant-based Milk
Tempeh (natural culturing and fermentation process that binds soybeans)

An Example of a Weekly Meal Plan

	Monday	Tuesday
Breakfast	Overnight oats	Stuffed apples
Lunch	Black bean salsa	Buddha bowl
Dinner	Green wrap	Jackfruit taco

	Wednesday	Thursday
Breakfast	Smoothie w/ side fruit	French toast
Lunch	Hummus w/ chips	Fruit and crackers
Dinner	Loaded avocado	Black bean burger w/ chips

	Friday	Saturday
Breakfast	Fruit bowl	Tofu scramble
Lunch	Chix pea salad	Trail mix
Dinner	Celery peanut butter	Chicken-less salad

	Sunday
Breakfast	Dry cereal and banana
Lunch	Avocado toast
Dinner	Penne w/ sauce

My 1300 Calorie "Fix"

This was something I tried for about a month recommended by my nutritionist. Helping to keep me on track and ble to set small goals to work toward. Of course I adjusted it to work with my busy lifestyle.

Fats - examples of 30 calorie servings

6 almonds
2 walnuts
2 pecans
1 teaspoon olive oil
6 black olives
1 teaspoon coconut oil

Fruit 50 calories per serving

2 cups grapes
1 cup watermelon chunks
1 cup strawberries
½ cup pineapple
1 small pear
½ small cantaloupe
1 banana
1 cup broccoli
1 cup green beans
1 cup asparagus
1 cup spinach
1 cup brussel sprouts

Gluten Only in Moderation

2 cups pasta
½ cup oatmeal
1 serving fiber cereal
whole grain bread

Carbohydrates In Moderation

baked potatoes
rice
pasta
starchy vegetables
bread

Breakfast

    2 servings protein
    1 serving carbohydrates
    1 serving fruit/ vegetable

Snack

    1 serving protein
    1 serving carbohydrates
    1 serving fruit / vegetable

Lunch

    1 serving protein
    1 serving carbohydrates
    1 serving fruit / vegetable

Snack

    1 serving protein
    1 serving fruit/ vegetable

Dinner

    2 servings protein
    1-2 servings leafy salad

The Raw Vegan
(fruits & vegetables)

Bananas Overload (milkshake)

4 -5 frozen bananas (depending on how thick you want it)
½ cup vegan (Enjoy Life brand) chocolate chips
2 cups plain almond milk.

In a blender, add milk, chocolate chips and one banana at a time for thickness.

Beets Me (juice)

3 beets or 1 can of beets
1 cup strawberries
1 cup raspberries
½ carrot
2 cups apple juice

Add all ingredients to blender on juice setting and serve over ice

Berry Good (smoothie)

½ cup frozen blueberries
½ cup frozen raspberries
½ cup frozen strawberries
½ cup frozen blackberries
3 cups acai juice

Add all fruit to the blender, then slowly pour acai juice to fruit and serve.

Blue Goddess (smoothie)
2 frozen bananas
2 cups frozen blueberries
1 cup spinach
1 can coconut water

Add all fruits, vegetables to blender and then pour in coconut water slowly to better control thickness

Bowl of Fruit (juice)

1 avocado
½ cup strawberries
½ cup pineapple
½ cup mango
½ cup banana
2 cups fresh squeezed orange juice

Add all ingredients to juice, blend and serve over ice.

Chocolate Covered Banana (ice cream)

1 tbsp cocoa powder
3-5 frozen bananas
3 cups chocolate almond milk

Add banana, cocoa powder, slowly pour in milk and blend. Then place in the freezer for 2-3 hours and enjoy. (optional add chocolate chips)

Green Day (juice)

2 avocados
1 frozen banana
1 can of pears or two fresh pears
1 cup fresh apple juice or fresh apples
4 kiwis
1 cup coconut water

Add all fruit to juice, blend and serve over ice.

Green Monster (juice)

1 cucumber
1 cup spinach
1 green apple
1 celery stick
1 avocado
2 cups coconut water

Add all fruit, vegetables in juicer and serve over ice. If using a blender add all fruits, vegetables then slowly pour in coconut water.

Strawberry Lemonade (juice or frozen pop)

2 cups frozen strawberries or fresh
2 cups lemon juice or 8-14 fresh squeezed lemons
1 teaspoon agave

Mash strawberries in the bowl, then add lemon juice then place in plastic popsicle sleeves. Place in the freezer (4hrs) then enjoy on a hot summer day.

Side Pieces (juice)

1 cup chopped spinach
1 cup chunks of pineapple
½ cup strawberries
½ cup kiwi
1 green apple (juice)
½ cup shredded carrot
½ cup cucumber
1 avocado
2 cups coconut water

Add all fruit, vegetables and place in juicer then serve over ice.

Nut Butter (smoothie)

4 frozen bananas
2 tablespoons of peanut butter
2 cups almond milk
(adding chocolate optional)

Add bananas, peanut butter, then slowly pour milk for your desired thickness and enjoy.

Peaches n Cream (smoothie)

1 cup canned, fresh or frozen peaches
1 can coconut cream
1 frozen banana
½ cup almond milk

Add fruit, coconut cream to the blender then slowly pour milk and serve in a chilled glass..

Strawberry Banana (ice cream)

1 cup frozen strawberries
4 frozen bananas
2 cups almond milk

Add fruit to the blender, then slowly pour in the milk in a bowl. Place in the freezer for about 4hrs then top with extra bananas for liking and enjoy.

Planet Earth

1 can of coconut water
1 1/2 cup mangos
1 cup spinach
2 bananas

Add all ingredients to the juice machine and serve over ice. If made in a blender add all fruit, vegetables and slowly pour in coconut water and serve over ice.

Sunrise (breakfast)

Tofu scramble

1 tub of tofu
3 cups diced tomatoes
½ cup chopped onions
1 clove of garlic
1 tablespoon of turmeric
½ teaspoon of black pepper
vegan cheese optional

Rinse all vegetables off first, then chop the tomato, onion, garlic and sauté in a pan with oil. Drain the excess water from the tofu with a paper towel. Add tofu in a pan with turmeric, black pepper and mash tofu (like a scramble egg). Cook to heat tofu and serve by itself or in a wrap for breakfast.

Pancake Skewer

2 cups banana flour
2 ½ cups almond milk
1 teaspoon vanilla
1 banana
5 strawberries
chocolate chips optional

Rinse strawberries and slice, peel bananas, slice them and set aside. Mix all the other ingredients in a large bowl. Heat frying pan on medium, spray with light cooking oil and the pour pancake mix . After they are done cooking, take a skewer, stack strawberry, banana and pancake. Top with whip cream and serve.

Tofu Scramble with Homefries

Tofu scramble with vegetables

Breakfast Potato

4 whole large white potatoes
½ chopped onion
1 clove of chopped garlic
1 cup vegetable oil
1 seasoning packet of sazon (Puetro Rican seasoning)
1 teaspoon black pepper

Heat vegetable oil on medium in frying pan, then wash, chop onion and garlic. Once oil is heated add potatoes, cook until golden brown and crispy(optional dipping sauce).

Avocado Toast

2 slices of bread or bagel store bought or homemade
1 avocado
½ onion
1 large tomato on the vine
1 lime
1 teaspoon olive oil
1 teaspoon black pepper
1 teaspoon of minced garlic optional
2 pieces of cilantro

First wash produce and then mash avocado in a bowl. Then chop the onion, tomato, cilantro and add to a bowl. Add remaining seasoning to the bowl and squeeze half lime over the spread. Toast your bread and spread on the avocado.

Fruit Bowl

1 kiwi
1 cup of blueberries, raspberries and strawberries
½ cup honeydew melon
2 cups grapes
1 vegan yogurt cup
½ cup granola
½ cup chai seeds
½ cup shredded coconut

Rinse all fruits in cold water, peel and cut kiwi. In a medium bowl add fruit, yogurt then lay shredded coconut, chai seeds and granola in a row. Then chill for an hour and enjoy.

French toast

2 slices bread of choice
2 tablespoons cinnamon
1 tablespoon vanilla
2 vegan egg (Just Egg brand a great substitute)
½ cup plant-based milk (I prefer walnut milk, for thickness)

Heat pan to medium, add butter then mix all three ingredients together in a bowl and let sit. Dip bread in mixture, place in pan and cook on both sides about 2 minutes each. Add cinnamon, powdered sugar, whip cream and some fruit to top it off.

Cheese Grits with Sauteed Vegetables

1 box of grits
5 pieces of kale
5 mushrooms sliced
½ onion sliced
2 tablespoons of oil
2 teaspoons black pepper
3 tablespoons vegan butter
2 cups vegan cheese
3 cups purified water
salt optional

Fill the pot with water, 1 teaspoon of butter and bring to boil then add grits. Once the grits begin to boil turn heat to low, more butter, black pepper and cover with lid. Place the frying pan on medium heat and add olive oil. Wash kale and dry with a paper towel, then roll the leaves and chop. Then slice onions and mushrooms. Once the oil is heated add vegetables and seasoning of choice. Once they're cooked down and tender then top over grits (add bacon bits or cook in with the kale to add another source of protein)

PBC (peanut butter, banana and chocolate sandwich)

1 banana
1 tablespoon peanut butter
½ bar melted chocolate
2 slices of bread of choice

Take ½ bar of vegan chocolate, melt in a small saucepan then spread on both pieces of bread. Spread peanut butter on one slice of bread, then slice the banana and place on bread . Heat frying pan on medium, close sandwich then add vegan butter to both sides and place in pan. Toast both sides of the bread. Remove from the pan, cut in half and serve. Great with a glass of plant based milk.

Stuffed Apples

2 apples (gala prefered)
8oz vegan cream cheese
½ cup granola, homemade or store bought
½ cup raisins

Preheat the oven to 350 degrees. Wash apples, then cut top of apples off and scoop out inside. Add a little lemon juice inside of apples, layer them with granola and cream cheese. Place apples in a pan, place in the oven and bake for 25 - 30 mins. Serve with ice cream or drizzle maple syrup.

Sweet Potato Pancakes

2 large sweet potatoes
1 cup banana
¾ cup almond or walnut milk
1 teaspoon maple syrup
1 teaspoon baking powder

Wash potatoes and boil. Peel and mash potato in a bowl and add other ingredients. Heat a frying pan with olive oil on medium then add pancake mixture and cook on each side for 2 mins. Add fresh fruit or maple syrup and enjoy with a glass of plant-based milk.

Stuffed Apples

No Bake Peanut Butter Oatmeal

1 cup peanut butter
3 cups rolled oats
½ cup raisins
½ cup agave or honey

Heat peanut butter on the stove, stir in oats and raisins until coated. Remove from heat and press firmly in a square pan (or make a firm ball). Refrigerate until cool and enjoy for breakfast or mid-day snack.

Overnight Oats

1 cup old fashioned oats
1 teaspoon natural vanilla
1 cup almond milk
2 teaspoons agave
optional 1 tablespoon nuts or ½ cup fresh fruit

Mix all ingredients together in a mason jar then place in the refrigerator overnight. Heat or eat cold in the morning.

Dip and Chip
(best served with wine)

Black Beans Salsa

2 cans black beans
1 can corn
3 tomatoes
1 onion
2 cloves of garlic
2 teaspoons vegetable oil
2 teaspoons apple cider vinegar
1 black pepper
5 stems of cilantro

Wash vegetables, dice tomatoes, onions and place in a bowl. Then add oil, apple vinegar, pepper and mix. Serve with chips or in a wrap with rice. This will make 3 16oz mason jars

Hummus

2 cans garbanzo beans
4 cloves garlic
2 teaspoons black pepper
4 teaspoons olive oil

Rinse beans and save the excess juice, place all ingredients in a food processor until it reaches a creamy mix(may need to add juice to thin out). Then enjoy with tortilla chips. Store in the fridge for about 2 weeks.

Black Bean Salsa

Mango Salsa

2 mangos
4 kiwis
2 avocados
1 pomegranate
5 stems of cilantro
1 lime

Wash all vegetables then cut mango, slice kiwis and avocados and de-seed pomegranate. Chop cilantro, mix all other ingredients in a bowl then squeeze lime and serve with tortilla chips.

Simple Guacamole

2 avocados
3 stems of ciltrano
1 tomato on vine
1 cup chopped onion
1 lime
½ teaspoon black pepper
2 teaspoons of olive oil
1 teaspoon of apple cider vinegar

Wash all vegetables, chop onion and tomato. Cut avocado and mash in a bowl until smooth and then add all other ingredients. Mix everything together, squeeze the lime over it and enjoy.

Spinach and Artichoke Dip

2 bags or fresh bundles of spinach
1 jar or 2 fresh artichokes
1 container toffi cream cheese
2 bags vegan cheese (prefer Go Veggie Mexican style)
1 teaspoon black pepper
1 clove garlic minced
(optional add ¼ cup almond milk to stretch the cream)

Preheat the oven to 400 degrees, wash spinach and artichoke in cold water. Mix spinach, artichoke, cream cheese, cheese, garlic and pepper. Place in an aluminum or glass pan for 30-45 mins. until light brown around edges (indication that cheese is melted). Serve with a baguette bread or tortilla chips.

Grass Fed
(salads as sides)

Avocado Salad with Strawberry Vinaigrette

2 avocados
1 grilled corn off the cob
2 cups of arugula (leafy vegetable bitter yet tart and pepper flavor)
1 tomato
½ cup onion
½ cup cucumber
½ cup cranberries
1 cup strawberries
½ mandarin oranges

Dressing -add 2 cups strawberries, 1 teaspoon agave, 1 tablespoons apple cider vinegar, 2 tablespoon olive oil, ¼ teaspoon black pepper, ¼ teaspoon pink hymilaya sea salt and set aside. Wash all produce, dice tomato, dice onion, slice cucumber, then slice strawberries and avocado. Lay arugula on the plate and begin to build your salad.

Cranberry Apple Salad

4 cups arugula
½ cup chopped onion
1 cup cucumber
1 cup cherry tomatoes
1 cup cranberries
1 apple cut apple (gala)
4 Nasturtium edible flowers (containing high vitamin c)
1 cup maple dressing

Wash all produce, then dry arugula with a paper towel and lay on the plate. Then chop onion, apple, slice cucumber then start layering everything on your plate. Now drizzle maple dressing and garnish with nasturtium.

Swiss Chard Boat

1 bundle Swiss chard
2 cups wild rice
1 can of black kidney beans
1 cucumber sliced thin
1 carrot shredded
1 diced tomato on vine
½ chopped onion
2 cups steamed broccoli

Wash all produce, lay out swiss chard to dry on paper towels. Cook rice as instructed on the package, then place chard on the plate and then put chopped vegetables on chard and fold in half. You can serve raw or sauté vegetables in olive oil. Mix oil, vinegar, salt, pepper and enjoy (or add your favorite dressing).

Chickenless Salad with Green Goddess Dressing

2 cups romaine lettuce
1 pack tempeh
1/2 cup tomato
½ cup onion
½ cucumber
2 tablespoons dried cranberry
4 sliced strawberries
¼ cup parmesan cheese
1 piece of toasted bread for homemade croutons

Dressing-Goddess dressing, mash 1 avocado, add 2 tablespoons olive oil, 1 teaspoons black pepper, 1 tablespoon apple cider vinegar, chop a few stems of ciltrano mix and set aside.

Tempeh-season with 1 pack sazon, 1 teaspoon black pepper, 1 teaspoon adbo, place in oat milk then dip in batter and fry

Preheat a frying pan on medium heat with olive oil and cook tempeh. Wash lettuce, dry with a paper towel and add to a bowl with other ingredients. Once everything is mixed well cut bread in small cubes, top salad and enjoy.

Cucumber Salad with Strawberry Vinaigrette

1 diced large tomato on vine (fresher and sweeter)
1 cucumber diced thin
1 carrot shredded
2 teaspoons oil
1 teaspoon black pepper
½ cup vegan mayonnaise, or mix avocado with olive oil

Dressing - add 2 cups strawberries, 1 teaspoon agave, 1 tablespoons apple cider vinegar, 2 tablespoons olive oil, ¼ teaspoon black pepper, ¼ teaspoon pink hymilaya sea salt and set aside.

In a large bowl add tomato, onions, cucumbers and carrots. In another small bowl add oil, mayo, pepper, salt and vinegar. Mix all ingredients together, place in the fridge for 2 hours and enjoy.
In a large bowl add tomato, onions, cucumbers and carrots. In another small bowl add oil, mayo, pepper, salt and vinegar. Mix all ingredients together, place in the fridge for 2 hours and enjoy.

Eggless Potato Salad

8 large potatoes
¼ cup mustard
½ cup relish
1 cup mayonnaise
2 tablespoons black pepper
3 tablespoons paprika
½ teaspoon pink himalaya sea salt

Wash the potatoes then place in a pot of water on the stove on medium heat. Once the potatoes boil, drain the water and let cool. After they've cooled, peel the potatoes and cut into small pieces. Mix the potatoes, other ingredients in a bowl and refrigerate for 30 minutes to an hour before serving.

Fancy Salad with Raspberry Vinaigrette

2 cups spinach
1 cup sprouts
1 diced tomato
1 cucumber
1 onion
¼ cup mandarin orange
¼ cup dried cranberries
(in season strawberries and apples too)

Dressing - add 2 cups raspberry, 1 teaspoon agave, 1 tablespoon apple cider vinegar, 2 tablespoons olive oil, ¼ teaspoon black pepper, ¼ teaspoon pink hymilaya sea salt and set aside.

Rinse all produce, then dice tomato, dice onion, slice cucumber. Add spinach to the plate, add other ingredients on top and drizzle oil and vinegar.

Strawberry Kiwi Salad with Strawberry Vinaigrette

1 cup onion
1 cup cherry tomato
1 cup shredded cucumber
4 cups romaine and arugula blend
1 kiwi
1 cup sliced strawberries

Dressing - add 2 cups strawberries (mash them well), 1 teaspoon agave, 1 tablespoon apple cider vinegar, 2 tablespoons olive oil, ¼ teaspoon black pepper, ¼ teaspoon pink hymilaya sea salt and set aside.

Rinse all produce, dry greens on a paper towel and chop onion. Then add sliced cucumber, strawberries and kiwi. Add green blend to plate, build other ingredients on top and drizzle dressing on top.

Strawberry Kiwi Salad with Strawberry vinaigrette

Taco Salad

1 cup cooked lentils, walnuts or groundless crumbles
1 diced tomato on the vine
1/3 cup onions
1 cup shredded lettuce
1 clove garlic
1 tablespoon taco seasoning
1 teaspoon black pepper
1 teaspoon onion powder
1 cup water
 about 2 handfuls of corn tortillas chips, soft wrap and or lettuce
 (vegan cheese sauce and sour cream optional)

Wash all produce first then dice tomato, onion, shredded lettuce and heat frying pan on medium. Put walnuts in the food processor and blend till fine. Add olive oil to cook walnuts for 10-12 minutes with garlic. Place chips on a plate, then add walnuts and other toppings.

Veggie Pasta Salad

1 box elbow macaroni
1cup broccoli
1 cup diced cucumber
2 cups diced tomato
1 cup diced onion
1 cup shredded carrot
1 cup of dressing (I prefer Just Mayo brand)
3 teaspoons mustard
¼ cup relish
1 teaspoon black pepper
1 teaspoon pink himalaya sea salt

Boil noodles of choice (I like elbow), then dice the cucumber, tomatoes, onions, broccoli and shredded carrots. Drain water from noodles and place in a bowl. Mix all the ingredients together in a bowl, place in the refrigerator for about 2 hours and enjoy.

Veggie Pasta Salad

Wrap it Up
(sandwich with chips)

Kale Chips

1 bundle of kale
½ teaspoon olive oil
½ teaspoon black pepper
½ teaspoon garlic powder
½ teaspoon of Pink Himalaya sea salt

Preheat the oven at 400 degrees, wash and lay the kale out on a paper towel to dry. Then lay on a sheet pan. Once dry add seasoning of choice and drizzle olive oil over the kale. Place in the oven for about 20 minutes (check often so it won't burn). Let cool and enjoy.

Chick Pea "Tuna" Wrap

1 can of chick pea
½ onion
1 stalk of celery
1 garlic clove
1 tablespoon black pepper
½ tablespoon vegetable oil
2 pieces of romaine lettuce
(carrot optional)
Serve on spinach or salad

Rinse the chickpeas, then place in a food processor and add garlic. Blend until creamy (I recommend taking the shells off beans first), then rinse celery and chop into small pieces. Place chickpeas, celery, oil, pepper in a bowl and blend well. Toast bread, lay lettuce on bread, add tuna mixture and close sandwich and enjoy.

Tofu Sandwich

1 avocado
½ tomato
½ onion
½ cup shredded lettuce
½ cup sprouts
1 teaspoon black pepper
1 teaspoon Old Bay seasoning
1 thin sliced tofu
1 tablespoon mayo
everything bagel for extra flavor

Preheat the oven to 400 degrees, take tofu out of the package, drain, cut in thin slices and season it. Spray the sheet pan with oil and bake tofu for 10-15 minutes. Toast bread, then spread mayo on bread and add tofu. Layer the veggies to build up your sandwich. Enjoy with chips and some infused water.

Tofu Sandwich

Green Wrap

½ cup black beans
1 cup wild rice
1 cup broccoli
½ cup cooked corn
1 large avocado
1 spinach wrap or chard

Cook rice, heat beans, corn and steam broccoli. After everything is cooked, place spinach tortilla wrap on a plate, spread avocado then add all the other vegetables and roll wrap up. Once wrapped and stuffed, cut in half and enjoy.

Lion MushroomWrap

1 avocado
1 cup shredded romaine lettuce
1 sliced tomato on vine
½ cup sprouts
½ cup onion
1 cup lion mushrooms
1 tablespoon avocado oil
½ teaspoon black pepper
tortilla wrap of choice
1 tablespoon olive oil
1 tortilla wrap

Rinse all vegetables, heat the frying pan on medium, add lion mushroom and onion. Add seasonings, cook until tender, add cheese to melt and place the lid over the pan. Now you're ready to build your wrap, place the tortilla on a plate, lay lettuce, tomato and the mushroom. Now your ready to roll, cut in half and serve

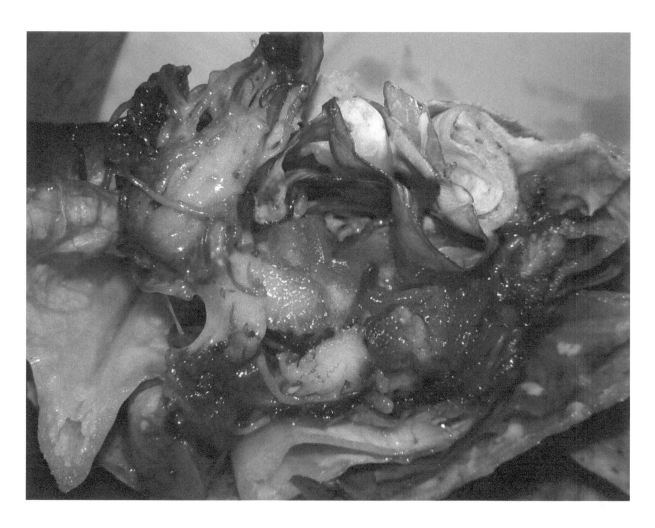

Lion MushroomWrap

Sundown
(dinner time)

Buddha Bowl

1 cup jasmine rice
1 cup corn
1 cup beans
1 cup broccoli
1 cup of corn
1 cup cooked Swiss chard
1 teaspoon black pepper
1 teaspoon Old Bay seasoning
2 tablespoons avocado oil

Cook rice in vegetable broth, sauté broccoli in avocado oil and heat all other vegetables. Once everything is heated add to bowl in sections, place sliced avocado on top and enjoy.

Curry Chickpeas

1 cup almond milk
½ cup coconut milk
½ cup rye flour
1 teaspoon black pepper
1 teaspoon paprika
½ chopped onion
1 can mixed vegetables (the lazy way)
1 chopped carrot
1 potato chopped small
1 can of chickpeas
1 can of green peas

Heat frying pan with olive oil, chop onion, garlic sautéed until soft and add all the other vegetables into the pan. Add coconut milk, almond milk, curry powder and let boil. Once at a boil cover, simmer low and cook for about an hour (once chickpeas are soft). Serve over red rice.

Curry Chickpeas

Egg Rolls

1 cup green cabbage, shredded
1 cup purple cabbage, shredded
2 cups shredded carrots
2 cups vegetable oil
2 teaspoons black pepper
1 pack Friedas Egg Roll Wrapper
duck sauce

Rinse all vegetables under cold water, then slice both cabbages and shred carrots. Pour vegetable oil in the pan, heat on medium then stuff vegetables in egg rolls. Once oil is hot, place egg rolls in and cook until golden brown. Serve with duck sauce.

Fried Cauliflower

1 bottle of Just Egg, walnut milk or oat milk (for thickness in batter)
1 cup cornmeal and rice flour
1 crown of cauliflower
1 tablespoon black pepper
1 packet sazon seasoning
1 tablespoon basil
1 tablespoon Italian seasoning

Place all seasoning in a bowl with flour and cornmeal mixture. Heat vegetable oil in a pan on medium and wash cauliflower. Then break the cauliflower apart into small pieces, dip in egg then place in flour mixture and cook. Cook until golden brown, place on paper towels to drain and enjoy.

Egg Rolls

Jackfruit Sliders

1 can of jackfruit in water or ½ of fresh jackfruit
1 bottle of bbq sauce
2 teaspoons Cajun seasoning
2 teaspoons black pepper
½ teaspoon onion powder
½ teaspoon garlic powder
8 mini buns

Coleslaw

½ head of purple and green cabbage
2 carrots
1 ½ cups vegan mayo
2 teaspoons black pepper

Rinse all vegetables in cold water, then chop cabbage in a bowl and then shred carrot. Place cut vegetables in a large bowl, mix in mayo and black pepper. Place in the refrigerator to chill until ready to top on a slider.

Preheat the oven to 450 degrees, drain, rinse the jackfruit and spread on a baking sheet. Mix the seasoning together in a small bowl then sprinkle them over the jackfruit evenly. Drizzle olive oil over the jackfruit before placing it in the oven with a timer at 40 mins. Take the pan out of the oven, break up the jackfruit into shreds and add bbq sauce. Then place back in the oven for another 20 minutes. Now you're ready to put your slider together so toast the bun then add jackfruit and coleslaw. Close it up and enjoy.

Jackfruit Bowl

½ cup canned jackfruit
1 bunch of broccoli
1 cup snap peas
1/3 cup carrots
3 cups of noodles (I prefer Asian style)
½ cup bbq sauce

Bring 4 cups of water to a boil, add noodles, wash all produce and shred carrots. Once noodles are boiled, drain, place in a bowl and steam broccoli. Sauté jackfruit in a frying pan with olive oil and cook until tender. Add bbq sauce over jackfruit, add all other ingredients over noodles and enjoy.

Moo-less Mac

1 elbow macaroni or Banaza 8oz box (chickpea pasta)
1/2 cup almond milk
2 cups vegan cheddar cheese (I prefer Wayfare)
1 1/2 cup vegan shredded cheese (I prefer Violife)
3 tablespoons of vegan butter or olive oil
1 cup block cheese (I prefer Daiya cheese)
1 tablespoon black pepper
3 tablespoons nutritional yeast
2 tablespoons paprika

In a large pot, bring pasta to a boil, once noodles are tender and drain. In a bowl mix all ingredients together well, leaving out ½ cup of shredded cheese. Preheat the oven to 400 degrees, place pasta in a baking pan and bake 30 mins. Last few minutes add more cheese to top off, cool and enjoy.

Moo-less Mac

Seitan Grinder

1 clove garlic
½ cup chopped onions
1 cup shredded lettuce
1 sliced tomato on vine
1 avocado
1 teaspoon black pepper
1 tablespoon mayo
2 tablespoons olive oil
1 tablespoon of Old Bay Seasoning
1 box seitan (I prefer Sweet Earth brand) or homemade
1 grinder roll or bread of choice (cheese optional)

Wash all produce then heat the frying pan with 1 tablespoon olive oil on medium heat, to begin sautéing garlic and onions. Then take mayo, avocado, black pepper, rest of olive oil and mix together to make a spread. Once veggies are tender add seitan with seasonings, toast roll, place on plate and add spread to each side of roll. Add lettuce and tomato, Seitan should be finished cooking in about 10 to 15 minutes (based on how well you want it cooked). Adding cheese is optional.

Stuffed Peppers or Tomatoes

4 peppers or tomatoes (whichever you don't stuff place inside)
1 clove garlic
1 shredded carrot
1 chopped onion
2 cups wild rice
1 teaspoon black pepper
1 teaspoon cumin
(optional vegan cheese, ground walnuts and Gardein Crumbles)

Preheat the oven to 350 degrees, wash all produce, cut the top off pepper or tomato and scoop out insides. Chop garlic, onion, shred carrots and sauté in a pan with some olive oil. Boil the water for   rice. Once rice is done add it to pepper or tomato and then add vegetables. Place in the oven on a lightly sprayed baking pan and bake for 25 -30 minutes. Top with cheese for the last five minutes.

Stuffed Mushroom

2 containers of whole mushrooms
1 bundle or 1 bag fresh spinach
1 teaspoon black pepper
3 bags vegan almond cheese (from Trader Joe's)
1 container vegan cream cheese

Preheat the oven to 400 degrees. Wash spinach, mushrooms and cut out stems. Mix spinach, cream cheese, black pepper and cheese. Place spinach mixture inside mushrooms, put in oven for 20-30 minutes in glass pan and 25 minutes in metal pan (will vary in baking dish). Enjoy as a nice appetizer.

Sushi Rolls

4 sushi wraps
1 cup cooked rice
1 cup shredded carrots
1 avocado
½ cup shredded cucumbers

Wash all produce, then take sushi wrap and lay on a bamboo board. Lay rice over seaweed, add carrots, cucumber and sliced avocado. Roll your sushi and slice into 1 inch pieces. Plate and drizzle with dressing or sauce of choice.

Shepherd's Pie

4 cups walnuts grounded (Gardein Crumbles for a lazy man's way)
2 cups fresh or 1 bag of frozen corn
½ cup vegan butter (Earth Balance, soy free)
8 potatoes
½ onion
6 mushrooms
3 cloves garlic

Preheat the oven to 350 degrees, boil potatoes, wash and cut mushrooms. Then lightly grease the pan with olive oil to sauté garlic, chopped onion and walnuts. Cook for about 15 minutes until golden brown. Rinse corn in cold water; now that the potatoes have boiled, drain, peel and mash. Add butter and milk for flavor. It's time to layer this pie so add your walnut crumbles, corn and mashed potato(top with cheese optional). Bake for about 25-35 minutes, the first 30 with foil and last 15 without. Let it set for 10 minutes then enjoy.

Baked Ziti

9 oz can of sauce or purée tomato
3 large green peppers
1 pint mushroom
½ cup chopped onion
2 garlic cloves
½ cup dried basil
½ cup dried Italian seasoning blend
1 cup rosemary
½ cup thyme
vegan cheese optional
meatless crumbles or ground walnut optional

Wash all produce, add all these ingredients to a big pot and bring to a boil. Once the sauce comes to a boil simmer on low for 5 hrs. Preheat the oven to 350 degrees, boil ziti and then mix all ingredients in a baking pan. Place in the oven for about 30 minutes, last 10 minutes add cheese and let cool serve with garlic bread. Don't forget to save your vegetable scraps to make a vegetable broth.

Baked Ziti

Vegan Pizza

1 cup spinach
1 diced tomato
1 diced onion
1 clove of garlic
6 mushrooms
1 jar tomato paste
basil, thyme, rosemary
1 cup water
(lazy toppings are garden crumbles and vegan cheese)

Homemade Dough

2 cups flour
2 tablespoons sugar
4 teaspoons baking powder
3 tablespoons vegan butter
¾ cup almond milk
(1 teaspoon salt optional)

In a large bowl mix together flour, sugar, baking powder. Then cut in butter, stir in milk to form dough.

Other suggested crusts optional:
    Trader Joe's Pizza Dough
    pita bread
    eggplant

Preheat the oven to 375 degrees then roll dough, top with your fresh vegetables and sauce. Cook for 20 to 25 minutes and enjoy!

Vegan Pizza

Buffalo Blue Cheese Tempeh Pizza

½ cup hot sauce (I prefer Red Hot)
1 cup blue cheese (I prefer Wayfare)
1 cup spinach
1 tablespoon olive oil
1 package tempeh
5 slices vegan cheese (I prefer Chaos)
dough, store bought or homemade

Homemade Dough

2 cups flour
2 tablespoons sugar
4 teaspoons baking powder
3 tablespoons butter
¾ cup milk
(1 teaspoon salt optional)

In a large bowl mix flour, sugar and baking powder. Then cut in butter and stir in milk to form dough .

Preheat the oven to 350 then place dough in a bowl and let rise for 15 minutes in the bowl. Slice tempeh thin, cook in a frying pan on medium heat and then toss in hot sauce. Roll dough onto sheet pan, spread blue cheese, spinach, then add cheese, top with tempeh. Brush olive oil on the crust of dough and bake for about 25 minutes.

Notes

Vegetable Bake

2 potatoes
1 carrot
1 onion
2 cups brussel sprouts
1 garlic clove
2 tablespoons olive oil
pepper, salt to liking

Preheat the oven to 450 degrees, dice potatoes, slice carrots, onions, brussel sprouts, squash and spread on a baking sheet. Add garlic, pepper, salt and any other season you like. Lightly drizzle olive oil over vegetables and bake for 45-60 minutes, depending on size. Serve over rice or add noodles.

Vegan Chili

1 cup of your homemade sauce
1 can of fresh, canned or frozen kidney beans
1 can black beans
2 cups frozen or fresh corn
3 tomatoes on vine
1 onion
1 garlic
3 teaspoons chili powder
1 cup vegetable broth
1 cup mushrooms
2 chopped carrots
(optional Gardein Crumbles)

Turn the crockpot on high, rinse all canned vegetables off and strain off excess water. Chop tomatoes, dice onion, carrot, garlic, mushrooms and add all ingredients to the crockpot. Then turn down to medium heat for about 3-5 hours then serve over rice or with cornbread.

Vegan Chili

Vegetable Fried Rice

1 cup corn
1/3 cup onion
1 cup snap peas
½ cup carrots
2 cups jasmine rice or noodles
2 tablespoons soy sauce

Wash all produce, turn wok on medium heat and add olive oil. Once oil is heated place all vegetables in wok and sauté. Once vegetables are cooked and tender add rice. Cook for about 7 minutes, add more oil if needed, plate and serve with sprouts on top.

Fried Cabbage

1 head of cabbage
½ cup avocado oil
3 tablespoons black pepper
1 shredded carrot
1 tablespoon pink himalaya sea salt

Chop cabbage, place in a strainer and rinse with cold water. While cabbage is being rinsed, turn the stove on medium heat with olive oil, then place cabbage in a pot and cover. Let the cabbage cook down for about 30 mins then turn on low until tender. Then add shredded carrots, black pepper, salt and cook for another 20 minutes.

Vegetable Fried Rice

Pesto Pasta

1 cup spinach
1 avocado
1 cup broccoli
½ cup walnut milk
2 tablespoons olive oil
½ teaspoon black pepper
½ teaspoon garlic powder
½ teaspoon Pink Himalaya sea salt
2 cups penne pasta

Heat a frying pan on medium heat and begin to saute broccoli. Then place a pot of water on the stove to boil for pasta. Now place all other ingredients in the food processor and blend well. Once blended add sauce to sauteed broccoli and let cook on low for 10 minutes. Place pasta in bowl and add pesto sauce and enjoy with nice piece of garlic bread

Quesadilla

1 cup ground crumbles or lion mushroom
½ cup onion
1 teaspoon black pepper
1 cup Follow Your Heart cheese
1 clove garlic minced
½ cup peppers
2 tablespoons sour cream
1 cup shredded lettuce
2 spinach tortilla wrap
2 teaspoons olive oil

Heat a frying pan on medium, add olive oil and wash all produce. Next dice onion, garlic, pepper, seasoning and place in a frying pan with crumbles or lion mushroom. Cook until veggies are tender, place in bowl, clean pan and return to the stove. Add oil, place tortilla in pan, add bowl mixture, cheese and close with other tortilla wrap. Allow both sides of the tortilla to get golden brown, place on a plate, serve with lettuce and sour cream.

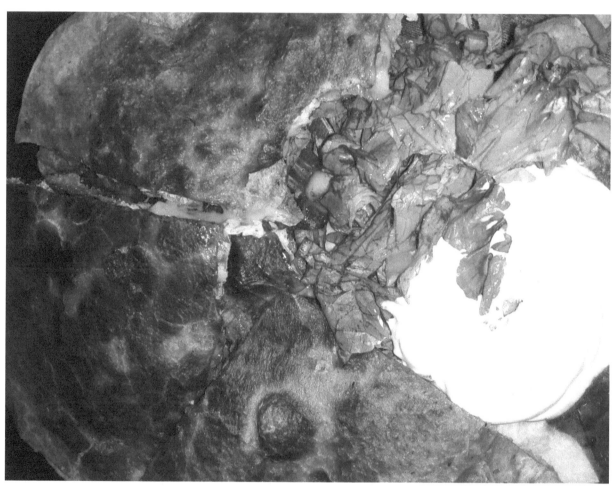

Quesadilla

Sweet Potato

6 sweet potatoes
1 teaspoon cinnamon
2 cups brown sugar
4 teaspoons I Can't Believe It's Not Butter or Earth Balance butter
1 tablespoon maple cream or maple syrup

Preheat the oven to 450 degrees. Wash sweet potatoes, cut into medium size pieces and place on a sheet pan. Place potatoes in the oven for 40-50 minutes. Mix sugar, cinnamon and butter in a small bowl. Continue to check and turn potatoes until golden brown and tender. Slice the potato down middle, add butter mixture and enjoy.

Loaded Avocado

2 large avocados
½ cup chick peas
1 tomato on vine (chopped)
½ small chopped onion
1 teaspoon black pepper
1/3 cup parsley leaves
2 tablespoons sour cream
½ cup shredded vegan cheese or a cheese sauce
1 cup walnuts (or Gardein Crumbles for the lazy man's way)
½ cup tortilla strips
2 tablespoons olive oil

Wash all the produce, chop tomato, chop onion and put mixture in bowl. Place walnuts in the food processor, then cook on stove medium heat . Cook until golden brown, remove seeds from avocado and place the ingredients in avocado. Top with cheese, sour cream and tortilla strips and enjoy.

Loaded Mashed Potatoes

7 large potatoes
½ cup vegan butter
2 tablespoons black pepper
2 cloves of garlic chopped
½ cup bacon bits
½ bundle broccoli
½ cup vegan shredded cheese (optional)
1 cup unsweetened almond milk

Wash all vegetables, place potatoes in a large pot of water and bring to a boil. Drain and peel potatoes and mash in a large bowl. Add almond milk, butter and mix. Add salt, black pepper, garlic, top with broccoli, cheese and bacon bits.

Loaded Nachos

1 cup shredded lettuce
1 diced tomato on vine
½ cup chopped onions
2 cups walnuts (or mushrooms)
3 cups full organic purple corn chips
½ cup chives

homemade cheese sauce

1 pkg. vegan cheese sauce (I prefer Daiya)
½ cup vegan shredded cheese (I prefer Aldi)
½ cup almond milk
1 teaspoon black pepper
1 tablespoon nutritional yeast

Add all ingredients to make cheese sauce in the pan and turn on low. Place walnuts in the food processor to blend well and cook walnuts on medium heat with olive oil in a pan. Don't forget to stir cheese sauce!! Place walnuts in a frying pan on medium heat and cook for about 7 to 10 mins. Now place chips on the plate and start building nachos up pouring cheese sauce last (optional to add sour cream).

Sweet Tooth

(treats you can't resist)

Apple Pie

7 large Gala apples
½ cup vegan butter
2 tablespoons cinnamon
2 tablespoons vanilla
½ cup brown sugar
Crust

homemade dough

2 cups flour
2 tablespoons sugar
4 teaspoons baking powder
3 tablespoons butter
¾ cup almond milk
(1 teaspoon salt optional)

In a large bowl mix together flour, sugar and baking powder. Then cut in butter, stir in milk to form dough.

Preheat the oven at 375 degrees, soak apples in baking soda and water to get residue off. Turn the saucepan on medium, add olive oil, slice and peel apples then place in a pan. While apples are cooking add cinnamon, sugar, vanilla and cook until tender. Once the apples are done, place in a pie pan, lay the crust on top and melt butter to spread with a brush around the edges of pie crust. Bake 50-60 minutes until golden brown and enjoy with whipped cream or vanilla dairy-free ice cream.

Apple Butter Bars

½ cup butter or apple butter
1 ½ cup flour
½ cup brown sugar
¼ cup applesauce
¾ cup apple butter
½ teaspoon baking soda
½ teaspoon apple pie spice
1 cup confectioners sugar
¼ teaspoon vanilla
2 teaspoons almond milk

icing
1 cup confectioners sugar
¼ teaspoon natural vanilla
1-2 teaspoons of almond milk

Preheat the oven to 350 degrees, beat butter until creamy then add half the flour, add the brown sugar, white sugar, applesauce, baking soda and apple spice together. Beat together until blended fine. Then beat in the remaining flour and spread onto a baking pan. Let bake for 25-30 minutes, cut into bars and drizzle icing. Let cool for 10 minutes and enjoy.

Chocolate Cupcakes

1 cup plain unsweetened soy milk
1 teaspoon apple cider vinegar
¾ cup sugar
1/3 cup canola oil
1 teaspoon vanilla
½ teaspoon almond milk
1 cup flour
1/3 cup dutch cocoa powder
¾ teaspoon baking soda
½ teaspoon baking-powder
¼ teaspoon fine sea salt

Preheat the oven to 350 degrees and whisk together milk and vinegar in a large bowl. Set aside for a few minutes for milk to curd. Add sugar, oil and vanilla until it's foamy. Sift flour, coca powder, baking soda, baking powder, salt and mix. Pour into the pan and let bake for 18-20 minutes.

Notes

Carrot Cupcakes

2/3 cup sugar
1/3 cup vegan butter
1 cup soy yogurt
1 teaspoon vanilla
2/3 cup flour
¾ teaspoon baking soda
¼ teaspoon baking powder
¼ teaspoon cinnamon
1 cup grated ginger
2 cups shredded carrots

icing
¼ cup butter
¼ cup cream cheese
¼ cup confectioners sugar
¼ teaspoon natural vanilla

Preheat the oven to 350 degrees. Mix sugar, vegetable oil, yogurt, vanilla and sift dry ingredients into a bowl. Then add to wet ingredients until smooth, fold in carrots, walnuts, raisins and bake for 26-28 minutes. While cupcakes are baking, beat butter and cream cheese, then add confectioners sugar and vanilla. Chill icing in refrigerator until cupcakes are done and cool about 10 minutes, apply icing and top with walnuts.

Carrot Cupcakes

Real Cocoa Rice Crispy Treats

1 box real cocoa cereal (I prefer Aldi or Mom's Best Cereal Rice)
1 bag vegan marshmallow (I prefer Dandies)
1 cup vegan butter or vegetable oil

Heat frying pan to medium heat and let butter melt, then add half the bag of marshmallows to melt. Once the butter and marshmallows are mixed, mix cereal in and turn heat off. Spread in a baking pan, let harden then enjoy with a glass of plant-based milk.

Mini Cinnamon Rolls w/ Apples

2 cups Bob Red Mill flour
2 tablespoons sugar
4 teaspoons baking powder
1 teaspoon salt
3 tablespoons vegan butter (Earth Balance prefered)
¾ cup almond milk

filling
4 tablespoons vegan butter (Earth Balance prefered)
1 cup brown sugar
3 teaspoons cinnamon

glaze
½ cup powdered sugar
¼ cup almond milk

Preheat the oven to 400 degrees. In a small bowl add together softened butter, brown sugar and cinnamon to form a crumbly mixture for filling. Sprinkle some on the bottom of the pan. Mix together flour, sugar, baking soda, and salt. Cut in butter and stir in almond milk to form a soft dough. Roll out dough on a lightly floured surface, roll up, and with a sharp knife slice into 12-14 rolls. Bake for 20-25 minutes. For glaze combine sugar and almond milk in a bowl and stir until smooth. Once rolls are finished, drizzle on glaze and serve warm.

Vegan Cinnamon Rolls with Apples

Lemon Cupcakes

1 ½ cups of flour
½ teaspoon baking soda
½ teaspoon baking powder
1/3 cup olive oil
1 cup soy or almond milk
¾ cups sugar
¼ cup and 1 teaspoon lemon juice
½ cup lemon zest

lemon buttercream frosting
½ cup vegan butter
2 teaspoons of cold soy milk
2 teaspoons lemon juice
1 ½ cups confectioners sugar

Preheat the oven to 350 degrees, mix swift flour, baking soda, baking powder, salt in a bowl and set aside. Whisk together olive oil, soy milk, sugar, lemon juice, lemon zest, and add to dry ingredients. Fill cupcake liners and bake for 18-20 minutes.

Plant-Based Brownies

3 large sweet potatoes
½ cup natural peanut butter
½ cup cocoa powder
1/3 cup maple syrup

Preheat the oven to 400 degrees and wash potatoes. Place sweet potatoes in water to boil. Once they are tender remove from heat and drain water. Once cooled, mix all other ingredients and place in a baking pan. Let cook for about 60 mins. Keep rotating the pan while cooking, then cool for about 10 minutes and enjoy.

Plant-Based Brownies

Pumpkin Chocolate Chip Cookies

1 cup flour
1 teaspoon cinnamon
¼ cup nutmeg
1 teaspoon sugar
1 teaspoon baking soda
½ cup pumpkin filling (fresh mashed or canned)
1 teaspoon flax seed (vegan egg substitute)
1 teaspoon natural vanilla
1 cup vegan chocolate chips

Preheat the oven to 350 degrees, mix dry ingredients together in a bowl. Then mix wet ingredients in another bowl and mix together. Chill in the refrigerator for 15 minutes or so. Spray sheet pan and bake cookies for 7-10 minutes.

Sweet Potato Pie

10 large sweet potatoes
3 cups pure brown sugar, or sweetener of choice
3 tablespoons vanilla
2 tablespoons cinnamon

homemade dough
2 cups flour
2 tablespoons sugar
4 teaspoons baking powder
3 tablespoons vegan butter
¾ cup almond milk
(1 teaspoon salt optional)

In a large bowl mix together flour, sugar, baking powder. Then cut in butter, stir in milk to form dough .

Preheat the oven to 375 degrees. Wash sweet potatoes, add to a pot of water on medium and bring to a boil. Remove from heat once tender, peel, then place in a mixing bowl. Mix brown sugar, cinnamon, and vanilla in a mixing bowl. Add to the mixture to the crust and apply egg wash or olive oil with a brush around the crust. Bake pie 50 - 60 minutes.

Peanut Butter Cookie

½ cup coconut oil
1 cup brown sugar
¼ cup almond milk
1 tablespoon vanilla
2 cups flour (I prefer Bob Red Mill unbleached flour in blue bag)
1 teaspoon baking soda
1 teaspoon baking powder
1 cup natural peanut butter

Preheat the oven to 350 degrees and mix brown sugar, almond milk, coconut oil and vanilla. Then slowly sift in flour and mix. Make teaspoon-size balls of dough, bake on a cookie sheet for 10-15 minutes and enjoy.

Double Chocolate Chip cookie

½ cup melted vegan butter
1 cup brown sugar
¼ cup almond milk
1 tablespoon vanilla
1 ½ cups flour (I prefer Bob Red Mill unbleached flour in blue bag)
1 teaspoon baking soda
1 teaspoon baking powder
¼ cup cocoa powder
1 cup chocolate chip

Preheat the oven to 350 degrees and mix brown sugar, almond milk, butter and vanilla. Then slowly sift in flour, cocoa powder and mix all ingredients together. Make teaspoon-size balls of dough, bake on a cookie sheet for 12-15 minutes and enjoy.

Chocolate Chip Cookie

½ cup coconut oil (best when melted)
1 cup brown sugar
¼ cup almond milk
1 tablespoon vanilla
2 cups flour (I prefer Bob Red Mill unbleached flour in blue bag)
1 teaspoon baking soda
1 teaspoon baking powder
1 cup chocolate chips

Preheat the oven to 350 degrees and mix brown sugar, almond milk, coconut oil and vanilla. Then slowly sift in flour and mix. Make teaspoon-size balls of dough, bake on a cookie sheet for 12-15 minutes and enjoy.

Coquito (Puerto Rican Coconut Nog)

1 15 oz can of cream coconut
1 7.4 oz sweetened condensed coconut milk
2½ cups almond milk
1 teaspoon vanilla
1½ cups Bacardi limited edition
2 teaspoons cinnamon
4 cinnamon sticks

Heat cream of coconut and condensed milk on medium until it comes to a boil. Once boiled add other ingredients and heat on low for 30 minutes. Let cool and place in the refrigerator. You can also blend cream and milk prior to heating to break up thickness. Once poured you can add more cinnamon on top. Drink within two weeks.

Chocolate Chip Cookie

Judy Gillian, my mentor, my agriculture guru, passed away as I was writing this book. She played a big part in 2 Cents Homegrown.

I met Judy in early 2017. She was eager to help me get a plot of land and begin farming. Her enthusiasm pushed me beyond my self-doubt and helped me realize that I had everything to gain and nothing to lose. She guided me to find funding and equipment, and as I was learning the fundamentals of farming, soil science, watering, and large- scale weeing, she pushed me beyond my comfort zone to expand and do more!!

When town bylaws were not favorable to agriculture, she fought the town. When this city kid got discouraged, she fought to put the wind back in my sails. She fought with determination and ambition.

Judy,with a smile and some tears, still hear you asking me why I haven't done more. I promise to keep farming, to keep agriculture alive. It was an honor to have crossed your path, and I miss you. This is dedicated to you, my friend.

My first plot with Judy's help 2019

Sunset from my plot

Priceless Moments

Cookie dough ready

Big E Fun 2019

Blueberry picking 2020

Asparagus festival 2019

Chamomile and Lavender 2020

My love for the animals

Entertaining a good friend(Julie)

First pick of 2020

Captured this beauty

This was my first book after 4 years being vegan, it was self published so there will be imperfections. After all the self doubt in putting this out. What better time than now covid-19 is showing us we need change in the world and in our bodies. I just wanted to share with you a little of my struggles and journey. I just hope you enjoy and learn a thing or two. You can find me on all social media platforms @2 cents homegrown Facebook, Instagram, Email 2centshomegrown@gmail.com or Youtube #veganfoodjunkie#